CW00449902

Braiding

JACKI WADESON

INDEX

This edition published in 1996 by Ultimate Editions

Ultimate Editions is an imprint of
Anness Publishing Limited
1 Boundary Row
London SE1 8HP

Distributed in Canada by Raincoast Books Distribution Limited

ISBN 1 86035 290 1

A CIP catalogue record of this book is available from the British Library.

Publisher: Joanna Lorenz
Senior Editor, Children's Books: Caroline Beattie
Photographer: John Freeman
Hair Stylist: Debbi Finlow
Designers: Tony Sambrook, Edward Kinsey

Printed and bound by Star Standard, Singapore.

Introduction

Doing your hair is such fun, and you'll be surprised to see how easy it is to create different styles. There are lots of things you can do whether your hair is straight, wavy or curly. All you need is a brush and comb, and as many brightly coloured ribbons, beads, bows, covered bands and flowers as you can find. Ask your mum if you can raid her sewing box: you'll find lots of interesting things you can use. Practise how to do a simple plait and ponytail first as these form the basis of many styles. It's great if you have a friend to help, then you can do each other's hair. Mix and match your colours to go with your favourite clothes. You can jazz up a plain T-shirt or give an outfit a whole new look just by changing your hair.

Happy braiding!

Jacki Wadeson

Contents

GETTING STARTED

BRAIDING FUN

Simple **P**lait

A three-stranded plait (also called a braid) is a lot easier than it looks.

1 Part your hair from centre front to the nape of your neck. Divide one half of your hair into three equal sections and hold the outer sections with your hands.

2 Cross the back section over the centre section. Use your fingers to make sure that the other two sections remain separate.

3 Now cross the front section over the centre section. It is important to pull all three strands of hair evenly as you work, so that your plait is straight.

4 Now you can see how the plait is beginning to form. Carry on plaiting, crossing the sections, right over centre and left over centre.

5 Hold the end of your plait about 5 cm from the end. Take a covered band and slip it over the end, then twist it back over as many times as you need to, so as to keep the plait secure.

6

Perfect Ponytail

A ponytail is one of the easiest styles to do. It keeps hair tidy and stops it getting into a tangle.

1 Brush your hair straight back using long sweeping strokes to make sure there are no knots. Tease any knots out by brushing gently from the bottom.

2 Place a fabric-covered band on your wrist, then pull your hair together with your hands at the back of your head.

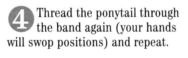

4 Thread the ponytail through the band again (your hands will swop positions) and repeat.

3 Slip the band off your wrist and over the ponytail. Hold your hair in one hand and twist the band with the other.

7

Twist & Roll

A really simple style that can be done in a jiffy, using a long fabric-covered band and a few twists of your wrists.

1 Brush your hair into a ponytail at the nape of your neck (see page 7). Secure in a covered band.

2 Take a long fabric-covered band and place over your ponytail. Cross over the ends over the top and hold them in your hands.

3 Twist the fabric band round the ponytail, right down the length of your hair, until you reach the ends of your hair.

4 Tuck the covered hair up and under, then cross the ends of the fabric band over one another to secure them.

Do the Flip

A nifty way to wear your ponytail – you just need a styler to flip it up and thread it down.

1 Brush your hair straight back and secure at the nape of your neck in a covered band.

2 Gently push the straight end of the styler down the centre back of your head, behind the covered band.

3 Hold the straight end of the styler and thread your pony-tail through the loop, then pull the styler down and your hair will flip through.

9

Beading

Add colourful beads – as many as you wish – to brighten up your hair.

1 Following the basic instructions given on page 6, braid a small piece of hair down one side of your face. Hold the ends together with a grip, then take a single bead and a small piece of glittery thread that you have folded to form a loop.

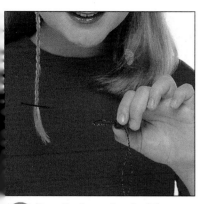

2 Pass the looped end of the thread through the centre of the bead. This is easiest if you make sure that the beads you use have quite large holes in the middle.

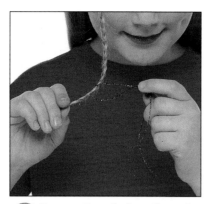

3 Remove the grip from the end of the braid and pass that through the loop of thread. Make sure you keep a firm hold on the bead, so it doesn't fall off.

4 Push the bead towards the braid, then pull the ends of the thread; the end of your braid will pull through the centre of the bead. Continue pulling until the end of the braid comes through the bead.

5 Wrap the thread around and around the end of your braid, making sure the strands lie flat. Carry on until you have covered about 1 cm of hair below the bead.

6 Cross over the ends of the thread, then repeat to form a knot. If necessary, cut the ends of the thread off, being careful not to snip the end of your braid.

TIP

Make sure you always keep your hair beads in a safe place away from babies or small children, who may think they are sweets.

Accessories

Clips, hairbands and floppy bows change your look in an instant.

2 Smooth your hair back and secure it with a zigzag band which fastens at the back of your neck underneath your hair.

3 Take the front section of your hair and clasp it in a band which has been decorated with short pieces of ribbon.

1 Scoop your hair up into a ponytail on top of your head and secure it in a band.

4 Scoop the front hair back from the ears to the crown and clip on a chiffon bow.

5 Add a neat velvet-covered band to dress up a low ponytail.

6 Secure the front hair back with a large tortoiseshell clip.

7 Hairbands come in all shapes and sizes and simply slide into place.

8 Take a small section of hair, twist it up and over and secure it in a mini clip.

9 Fine ribbon bows make tiny braids look extra special.

13

Bouncy Bunches

Any length of hair can be scooped up into pretty bunches. Add bright ribbons in fun colours for every day and fairy bows for party time.

TIP
Gift-wrap ribbon is ideal for making bows and covering grips.

1 Part your hair in the middle from front to back. Put a covered band over one hand, so that it sits on your knuckles (this makes it easy to slip over your bunch) and hold one half of your hair in the other hand.

2 Slip the bunch right the way through the covered band, holding your hair tightly with one hand and using your thumb to pull the band tight.

3 Twist the covered band round once, then put your fingers through the loop and pull the bunch through. Do this again until the band is tight enough to hold your hair.

4 Take a short piece of ribbon and tie it round the bunch, then make a bow. Repeat for the other side.

5 For fairy bows, twist thin ribbon round the top half of a grip, starting at the open end. Tie a tiny bow at the end of each grip. Use lots of different colours and simply push the grips into place round your hairline.

Heidi Hi

1 Part your hair in the middle from front to back. Comb half over one shoulder and divide into three equal pieces. Then plait right down to the ends of the hair.

2 Take a towelling band and push it over one hand so that it sits on your knuckles, whilst holding the end of the plait in the other hand. Don't let go or your plait will unravel.

3 Comb the other half of your hair over to the front of your shoulder and plait in the same way. Try to keep your plaits even by pulling equally on each section of hair.

4 Secure the end of the plait in a towelling band, as before, twisting to make sure it is tight enough to hold your plait.

5 You can either leave your plaits down or pin them on top of your head with a novelty slide.

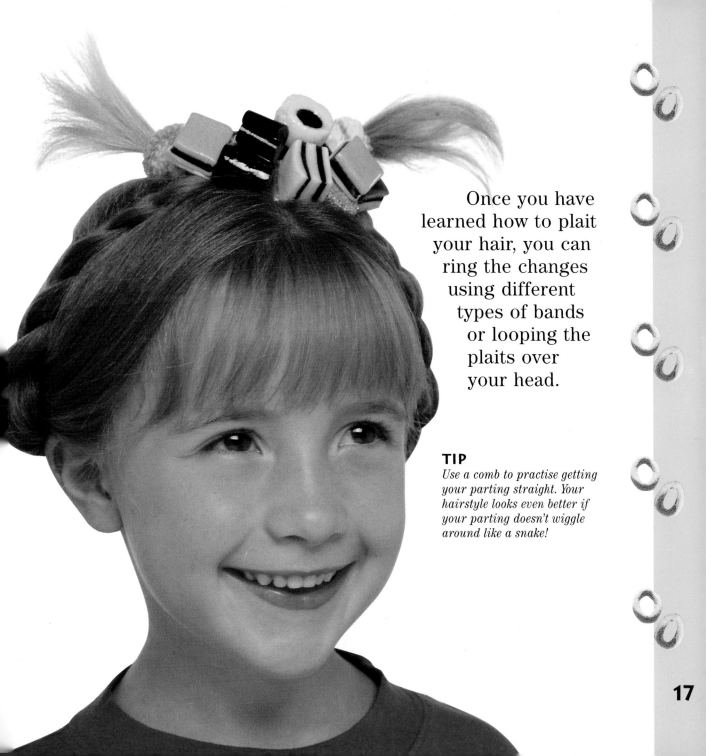

Once you have
learned how to plait
your hair, you can
ring the changes
using different
types of bands
or looping the
plaits over
your head.

TIP

*Use a comb to practise getting
your parting straight. Your
hairstyle looks even better if
your parting doesn't wiggle
around like a snake!*

Topsy Turvy

A topknot is great if you are growing out your fringe because you can catch in all those little ends that tend to stick out.

TIP
You can twist ribbons together for a really unusual hairband. Choose colours that match your clothes.

1 Brush your hair through to make sure you haven't got any tangles. Use the thumb of each hand to divide off the top section of the hair from your ears up to the top of your head.

2 Push a fabric-covered band over the fingers of one hand so that it rests on your knuckles, and clasp the topknot of hair in your other hand.

3 Slip a band over the hair and twist it, ready to repeat. Be careful not to let go of the topknot while you are twisting the band round your topknot.

4 Twist the band round again in exactly the same way. If it feels a little loose, then twist again until the topknot feels nice and firm. The number of times you need to twist depends on how big your band is.

5 You can dress up your topknot by taking two lengths of different-coloured thin ribbon and placing them around your head like a hairband. Simply tie the ends at the back of your neck, under your hair, where no one can see.

French Fancy

Straight bob-length hair looks great with small braids when they are cleverly twisted to give a trendy teen style. An unusual hair slide (we found a beautiful pair of elephants) adds the perfect finish.

1 Part off a small band of hair on the top of your head. Lift the front of this section and start braiding. As you cross the strands, bring a little more hair into the outer strands and work into the braid.

TIP
You can decorate plain slides by sticking pictures or buttons on them.

2 Take a small section of hair at the side of your head, in front of your ear, and braid from the roots to the ends. When you reach the ends, secure in a covered band.

3 Take another small section of hair at the other side of your head in front of your ear and braid in the same way, until you reach the ends. Secure in a covered band.

4 Take the two side braids and lift them onto the top of your head. Secure these, and the end of your top braid, in a large slide which will cover all the ends.

5 For a quick change, tie the ends of the braids in a fabric-covered band and divide the back hair into two neat little bunches with matching fabric-covered bands.

Beaded Braids

1 Part your hair in the centre, then take a small section of hair and divide into three equal strands. Begin to braid, working down from the roots to the ends. See page 6 for full directions.

2 Slip the beads over the end of the braid, as shown on pages 10–11. Attach a second bead in the same way and bind the ends with thread so the beads don't fall off.

3 Make as many more braids as you would like; we did three on each side. Make sure that you put the beads on at the same level on all the braids.

4 Brush the loose hair up high on the crown of your head and secure with a fabric-covered band. Brush the ponytail through so it's nice and smooth.

Tiny braids with beads threaded through the ends look difficult to do but are so easy. Bead just a few braids around your face or ask a friend to help you do them all over your head.

5 Make sure the beads and the fabric-covered band match or contrast nicely with your clothes.

6 Instead of using beads, try binding each braid with fine ribbon and finishing the ends with tiny bows.

TIP
Hair beads should have large holes in the centre so the braid slips through easily. You can usually find this type of bead in the button and bead departments of big stores.

Tiny Twists

Finely braided hair need not look the same every day. It can be twisted into tiny coils and brightened up with multi-coloured covered bands.

TIP

Fine braids like these can be left in the hair for weeks but it is best to remove hair accessories at night so they don't pull your hair or get tangled up.

24

1 Take about six fine braids in one hand and twist them together. You will find that the hair starts to roll back on itself and begins to form a coil.

2 Continue twisting, allowing the hair to coil round the finger of your other hand then carefully tuck the ends of the braids in, so the hair feels secure.

3 Push a small covered band over the first two fingers of one hand and use the other hand to hold the coil of hair. Carefully slip the band over your hair and push it down so the braids are held tight.

4 Make as many more twists as you want. We did four at the front and one in the centre of the back, but if you would like more simply use less hair for each one.

Racy Ribbons

Plaits look really good if you include ribbons as you go. At the ends tie each ribbon into a bow for a really beautiful cascade of colour.

TIP
Cut ends of ribbons on a slant to stop them fraying.

26

1 Part your hair in the centre and brush it through. Gather up the hair at each side and use a covered band to secure in bunches. Make the bunches at about ear level.

2 Take three lengths of ribbon, each of a different colour. Pull the ends halfway through the band, then tie them onto it once. Make sure the ends are roughly even.

3 Divide the hair into three strands and put two matching pieces of ribbon with each one. Now begin plaiting as normal right down to the ends.

4 Secure the end of the plait, including the ribbons, in a covered band. Now take each pair of matching ribbons and tie them in a bow. Plait and tie the other side.

5 You could always pop on a matching hairband and add a bow at the top of each plait.

27

Braids & Bows

Simple braids can be used in many different ways. See how two can be tied at the back of the head in a pretty bow, while tiny front braids can be decorated with a few small beads.

TIP

You could make a multi-coloured beaded band yourself. Thread beads onto lots of tiny lengths of cord and then tie them round a covered band.

28

1 Part your hair in the centre then take a small section of hair from one side. Start braiding near the roots and work all the way down to the ends. See page 6 for full details on how to braid.

2 Take a small section of hair from the other side of your head and braid in exactly the same way. Secure the ends in a covered band, twisting and wrapping the band around until it holds tight.

3 Take the braids round to the centre of the back of your head. Tie them together with a small piece of ribbon and loop it into a bow.

4 Braid two more sections of hair, so that each one hangs in front of your ear. Thread three different coloured beads onto each braid. (See pages 10–11 for details.) It looks nice if at least one of the beads matches your ribbon bow.

5 Finally, brush your hair (taking care not to spoil the braid or the bow) for a sleek finished look.

Banded Bunches

Keep your bunches tidy by wrapping bands of colour round them all the way to the bottom.

TIP

Design your own motif bands by sewing novelty buttons onto towelling bands.

1 Part your hair in the middle from front to back. Put a covered band over one hand so it sits on your knuckles, then slip it over this section of hair. Twist it back over until it's tight. Repeat for the other bunch.

2 Take two towelling bands (we used ones with little piggies on) and slip one over each bunch. You may need to twist them twice so they hold nicely.

3 Take two more different coloured towelling bands and slip a bunch through each band, about 5 cm from the first band.

4 Take more coloured bands and continue adding them to your bunches, always about 5 cm from the last, until you run out of hair, or bands!

5 Make sure the bands are at the same level all the way down both bunches. Why not clip pretty slides into the hair above each bunch?

Pretty Ponytail

1 Tip your head forward and brush your hair from the back of your neck right to the ends. Make sure there are no tangles or knots. It is easiest if you use a brush with wide spaces between the bristles.

2 Take hold of your hair with one hand and run the fingers of your other hand through your hair to make sure it is smooth. Keep hold of your hair and lift your head up.

3 Put a fabric-covered band over the knuckles of one hand, then pull your hair though the band. Twist the band and pull your hair through again until it is tight enough.

4 Add two more fabric-covered bands above the first one so that you get lots of height.

5 Use different coloured covered bands, as it looks good if the colours cross over and form a pattern. Pin little net flowers in place with grips to add an extra splash of colour.

A really high ponytail,
right on the top of
your head, makes you
instantly taller and
is one of the easier
styles to do.

TIP

You can get fabric flowers in the sewing
departments of large stores. Push a grip
into the back of each flower to help you
to fasten the flowers into your hair.

33

Ribbon Roll

1 Use a comb with widely spaced teeth to help you smooth your hair up onto the top of your head. Hold your hair with one hand and put a covered band over the other hand. Twist the band round your hair to make a ponytail.

It's easy to make very curly hair look neat and tidy if you plait a high ponytail with ribbon and twirl it into a roll.

34

2 Plait the ponytail from the top right down to the ends and secure the ends with another covered band. You could leave your hair just like this if you wanted to.

3 Take a length of the ribbon and slip one end under the covered band at the top of your head and pull through, so the ends are even. Bind the ponytail with the ribbon right down to the ends.

4 Take the ends of the ribbon and plait in one hand and roll the lot round on itself to make a bun. Use one or two grips to secure it in place but allow the ends of the ribbon to fall free.

5 We added a dark blue, pale blue and white cord hairband to change the look into one ideal for parties. A hairband is useful for keeping your hair off your face.

35

Triple Twist

1 Brush your hair into a low ponytail at the nape of your neck. Make sure the front is really smooth with no ends sticking out.

This is a perfect style if your hair is thick and wavy. The hair is divided into three and braided, then the three braids are formed into one. It looks complicated but is so easy to do.

TIP
Look in your mum's sewing box for oddments of fabric and ask her to help you make your own fabric bands.

2 Divide the ponytail into three equal sections. Take the first one and braid it from top to bottom. Look again at the instructions on page 6 if you can't quite remember how to braid.

3 When you get to the end of the braid, secure it with a covered band. Braid the other two sections in exactly the same way. You now have three braids to work with.

4 Take the three single braids and plait them together in the same way as before. Your hair will form into a thick plait that looks like a twist of hair.

5 Simply twist a covered band to hold the hair in one place. Or add two multi-coloured chiffon hair accessories to each end of the twist for a different look.

37

Pony Princess

Here the top section of your hair is smoothed back and the rest of the hair held by cute towelling bands to give a multi-coloured ponytail.

1 Brush your hair so there are no tangles or knots. Then use your thumbs to divide off the top section of your hair. Hold this section tightly with one hand.

2 Use a towelling-covered band to secure this top section of hair. You may need to twist once or twice so the band is tight enough to hold the hair properly.

3 Gather all your hair together at the nape of your neck and secure it in another towelling band of a different colour. You may need to twist it again so it's tight enough to stay in place.

TIP
Covered bands like these are made from flexible wire sewn into the edge of a long strip of fabric.

4 Take another coloured band and do the same thing again. The bands should sit neatly next to one another, so push them together.

5 Add another coloured band further down the ponytail. Or take a bendy fabric band, place it round the back of your head and bring the ends up on top in the front. Twist the ends into a circle to hold the band in place.

Be-Bop Bunches

High bunches like these are really easy to do on bob-length hair, and you can twist a section with ribbon for a really grown-up look too.

1 Part your hair in the centre and brush your hair so it is really smooth. Take a small section at one side and brush again. You can experiment to see how large a section you'd like to use.

TIP
To make your hair shiny always use cool water for the final rinse after you shampoo your hair.

2 Tie this small piece of hair in a band. We used crocheted silky bands in multi-colours which look really good.

3 Twist the band until it is tight enough to hold the hair in place. Repeat for the other side.

4 Divide off a small section of the hair from one of the bunches and slip the end of the ribbon halfway through the covered band. Twist the ribbon around your hair and tie the ends in a bow.

5 For that extra-special look, push grips through tiny fabric flowers of matching colours and use them as pretty accessories near one of the bunches.

Bobbie Braids

1 Divide the top section of your hair into two sets of braids. Take one section in one hand and slip a band over the other hand. You can use a plain band or one with beads attached to it.

2 Slip the band over the braids, twist round and slip the braids through the band again until it is tight enough to hold. Try to position the beads so they are at the front.

3 Take another band and tie it around the ends of the braids, twisting round and round until it is tight enough to hold. Again, position the beads so they are at the front. Repeat with the other side.

4 Take all the back braids in one hand and slip over another covered band close to the back of your head to make a ponytail.

TIP
You can make beaded bands like the ones we used by threading about eight beads onto shirring (thin) elastic and tying onto plain bands.

42

Braiding hair all over the head is a traditional and practical way to keep it neat and tidy. Adding pretty accessories lets you ring the changes each day.

5 Tie the end of the ponytail in a matching band to form a little tail.

6 Twist both the side ponytails into each other over the top of your head.

43

Mini Ha Ha

1 Part the hair in the centre and split off a section on one side. Braid as described on page 6 and then secure the ends in a covered band.

Mid-length hair can be triple-plaited and then bound at the ends with multi-coloured bands.

TIP

If you find your hair is flyaway ask your mum if you can borrow a silk scarf. Use the scarf to cover a bristle brush and stroke it over your hair. The static electricity, which makes hair wispy, magically disappears.

2 Make five more braids in exactly the same way. There should be one either side at the front, two behind your ears and two at the back.

3 Gather three braids together at one side and then plait these from roots to ends. The plait will be bulky to work with but is still easy to do. Secure with a covered band.

4 Repeat for the other side, working exactly as before. Secure with a covered band, pushing it up a little way so it covers the previous bands and makes it look as if the braids have been bound.

5 You can also add a hairband and bind the braids with fine matching or contrasting ribbon, finishing off with a bow.

Clever Cornrows

Cornrow braids look brilliant in bunches
and are ideal for beading and adding bows.

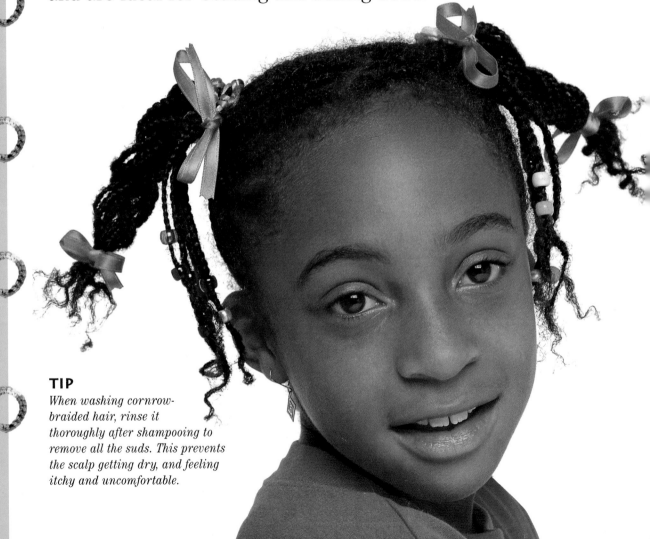

TIP

*When washing cornrow-
braided hair, rinse it
thoroughly after shampooing to
remove all the suds. This prevents
the scalp getting dry, and feeling
itchy and uncomfortable.*

1 Braid tiny sections of hair working flat to the head. You will need the help of your mum or a friend to do the back and sides. Be patient as it will take some time.

2 Divide the crown hair into two equal bundles of braids. Take one bundle in your hand and secure in a covered band, then repeat for the other side.

3 Gather up all the braids at the back into one hand. Take a covered band and slip it over, twist the band and repeat until it is tight enough to hold the ponytail.

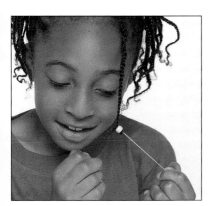

4 You can add two beads to each braid, or just on some. If you want instructions on how to do this, see pages 10–11. You could use lots of different beads on each braid or choose them to match your clothes.

5 You can also add tiny bows to the tops and bottoms of the bunches of braids. Use lots of thin, colourful ribbons for this.

Top & Tail

A simple plait takes on a party look if it is topped and tailed with fabric bands.

1 Brush your hair back from your face so it is really smooth and flat. Clasp the ponytail in one hand not forgetting to make sure that it is tangle-free too.

TIP

If you find you have lots of little pieces of hair sticking out then simply wet your hands and smooth over your hair to lay them flat.

48

2 Take a fabric-covered band and push it over one hand so it rests on your knuckles. Pass the ponytail through the fabric band, twist and turn until it is tight enough to hold your hair firmly.

3 Divide the ponytail into three equal sections and plait it from top to bottom. Work right down until you are 5 cm from the bottom.

4 Take a matching fabric-covered band and use it to secure the end of the plait. You may have to twist it up to three times to make sure it is tight enough.

5 The result is a decorative and neat plait. For a more grown-up look, twist the plait round into a bun and secure it with a covered band. Add three grips decorated with rosebuds in a colour to match.

49

Tufty Topknot

This fun style is really easy to do and is ideal for cornrow-braided hair.

1 Scoop all the front braids together and hold them in place with one hand. Take a covered band in the other hand then slip it onto the braids. Twist to secure.

2 Divide the bunch of braids into three equal sections and twist each set together to form a tuft of braids. Twist the ends together.

3 Gather all the back braids together and secure them in a covered band. Try to do this in the centre of the back of your head so it looks neat.

TIP

If you have a plain bow you can make it extra special by sewing on some unusual beads or buttons. Ask your mum if you can look in her button box for something suitable.

50

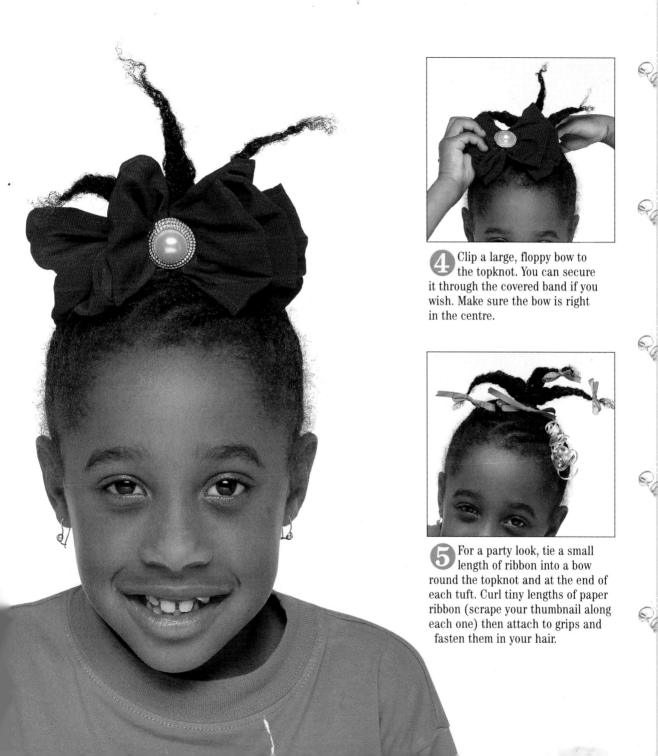

4 Clip a large, floppy bow to the topknot. You can secure it through the covered band if you wish. Make sure the bow is right in the centre.

5 For a party look, tie a small length of ribbon into a bow round the topknot and at the end of each tuft. Curl tiny lengths of paper ribbon (scrape your thumbnail along each one) then attach to grips and fasten them in your hair.

51

Wonder Waves

Straight hair can be changed into a mass of waves by using fabric curlers, but you do need to leave them in overnight to get the best result.

1 Take a fabric curler and fold it in half to grip a section of hair between the two pieces. Pull the curler right down to the bottom of the hair.

2 Wind the fabric curler up the hair from the ends towards your head. Do this slowly and make sure you don't let go of either end of the curler.

3 When you can wind no further, take the ends of the fabric curler and bring them both together, then cross them over. This is so that they hold the hair in place.

4 Repeat all over your head. Remember, the bigger the sections of hair you wind, the looser the wave will be. For really tight curls, take only small sections and use lots of curlers.

5 Leave your curlers in overnight. They are very soft so they won't keep you awake!

6 In the morning remove each curler and use your fingers to 'rake' through each wave. You could also scoop the front hair back and secure it with a sunflower slide.

TIP
You will get an even curlier effect if your hair is just very slightly damp. But remember never to go to bed with wet hair.

Teeny Bopper

1 Lift a section of hair from the front to the top of your head and then use a bristle brush to smooth the front of your hair. Do not brush through the length of your hair or you will pull the waves out.

2 Take a large covered band (one that will wrap round lots of times) and use it to secure the top hair. Make sure you do this right in the middle, because you don't want your topknot to be lopsided.

3 Take a section of hair at one side and fasten it with another large covered band in a different colour. Loosen the waves with your fingers, but don't brush or comb the length of your hair.

4 Do exactly the same on the other side using another covered band in a different colour. You can, if you wish, secure more bands like this at the crown.

54

Once you have waved your hair, you can create lots of other looks. Here, a trio of bands tames the waves and gives a fresh new style.

TIP

If you want to keep your waves for as long as possible, only rake through them with your fingers or use a wide-toothed comb.

55

Braided & Bound

Long straight hair can be braided then wrapped with different coloured ribbons for a really snazzy style.

56

1 Take small sections of hair and braid them tightly from roots to ends. See page 6 for full instructions on how to braid. You may need a friend to help you to braid the hair at the back.

2 Secure the end of each braid by wrapping with fine colourful thread. Wrap it round a couple of times before tying into a tight knot. Snip off any long ends, but be careful not to cut your hair.

3 Take a piece of narrow ribbon and fold it in half. Tie the ribbon to the top of the braid, then bind downwards by crossing the ribbon over and over, first at the front of the braid, then at the back.

4 Continue binding until you reach the end of the braid and tie the ends of the ribbon. Repeat until you have bound all your braids. You may need a helping hand to do the braids at the back.

5 Scoop up the braids on the top of your head and bind them into a topknot with narrow ribbon.

TIP

Fine ribbons can be left in your hair overnight because they are soft and won't pull your hair.

57

Crimping Crazy

1 Divide your hair into fine sections and braid it from the roots to the ends making the braids even and quite tight. The smaller the sections are, the finer the finished crimp will be.

2 Secure the end of each braid with a piece of thread, wrap it around two or three times and then tie the ends into a little knot. If you prefer, you can use very small covered bands.

3 Leave the braids overnight to set your hair into its new shape. You can lightly mist your hair with water if you wish but don't go to bed with wet hair.

4 In the morning carefully unravel each braid, loosening it with your fingers as you go.

TIP
Crimps will stay in your hair until you next wash it.

Big girls use crimping irons to create ripples in their hair but you can get the same effect by braiding your hair and leaving it overnight to set.

5 You can, if you wish, gently comb through using a wide-toothed comb or a brush with widely spaced teeth.

6 Keep your hair away from your face with a multi-coloured hairband.

Double Dazzle

Once you have crimped
your hair you can create
different styles with it.

1 Gently brush through your hair
but don't tug or pull too much
or you will loosen the crimps. Divide
off a section of your hair at the front
and hold it tightly in one hand.

TIP

*Paper flowers which are used
to decorate presents make
perfect hair accessories. You
can find them in stationery
shops or large stores.*

60

2 Take a covered band and place it over the knuckles of the other hand. This makes it easier to secure the bunch. Do not let go and keep the bunch tight to your head.

3 Pull your hair through the band, then twist the band and pull the hair through it again. Repeat until it is tight enough to hold the hair in place. Push the band close to the top of the bunch.

4 Repeat for the other side, making another bunch in exactly the same way. Try to make sure you use about the same amount of hair in each bunch.

5 Smooth the bunches down with your hands or a soft brush, but don't brush too hard! You could also take another section of hair on your crown and fix it in a covered band.

Plaited Flips

Plaits can be bound tightly with cord for a really unusual style.

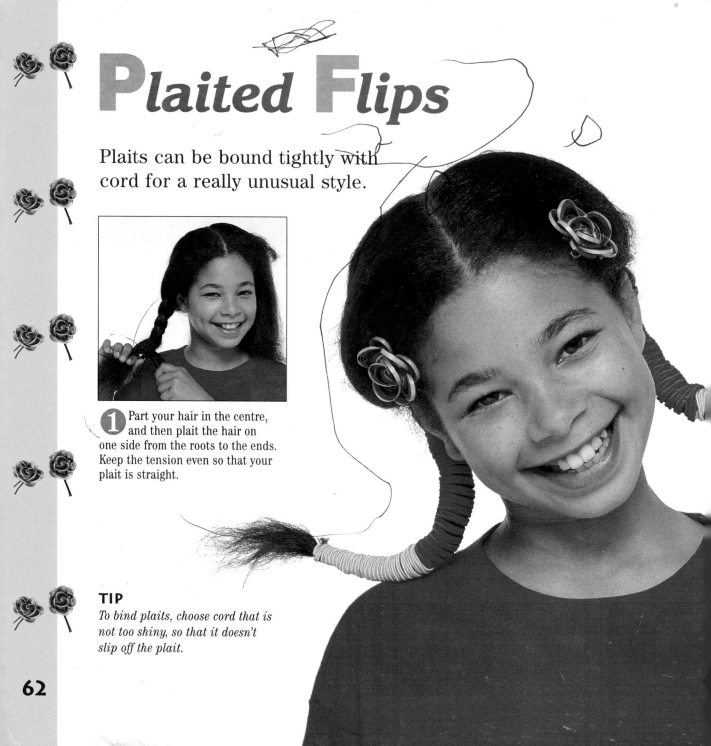

1 Part your hair in the centre, and then plait the hair on one side from the roots to the ends. Keep the tension even so that your plait is straight.

TIP
To bind plaits, choose cord that is not too shiny, so that it doesn't slip off the plait.

2 Secure the end of the plait in a covered band, twisting it back until it is tight enough to hold. Repeat, making a plait in exactly the same way for the other side.

3 Take a piece of fine cord and, starting at the top, bind the plait by wrapping the cord around and around it. Keep the circles of cord close to one another.

4 Half way down your plait, you can change the colour of the cord. Hold the ends of the first and second colours against the plait and bind the new colour tightly round the ends. Continue working right down to the end of your plait, and secure the end of the cord by tucking it into the covered band.

5 Add two flowers or matching slides to either side of your head, at the front or above the plaits.

63

ACKNOWLEDGMENTS

The Publishers would like to thank the following girls for modelling for this book:

Lauren Andrews, Charley Crittenden, Kimberley Durrance, Terri Ferguson, Sophia Groome, Nicola Kreinczes, Elouisa Markham, Tania Murphy, Lucy Oliver, Kim Peterson, Alexandra Richards, Leigh Richards, Kate Yudt.

The Publishers would also like to thank the following for lending hair accessories, brushes, combs and other equipment:

Boots; Head Gardener, Knightsbridge; Lady Jayne; Mason Pearson, Kent; Molton Brown; Tesco.

This book is designed for children between the ages of 8 and 12. All beads, bows, threads and hair accessories should be kept out of reach of babies and small children.

0900 1 22 99 88

A) The EAR